Yellow

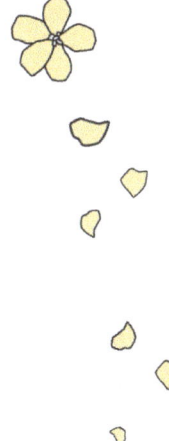

by Chelsea Hui

illustrated by The Colour Study

Yellow copyright © 2019 by Chelsea Hui. All rights reserved. No part of this publication may be reproduced, distributed, or transmitted in any form or by any means without written permission except for the use of brief quotations in a book review.

ISBN: 978-0-9876340-2-3

To Janice -
for teaching me how to dream,

And to my parents -
for helping me make them a reality.

Trigger Warning:

The contents of this book contains references to racism, sexism and sexual assault.

Please check top right corner of each page for appropriate content warnings.

Dear Reader,

To be completely honest with you, the journey to getting *Yellow* to where it is today has been extremely difficult. There have been countless setbacks over the last few years, some of which almost caused me to let go of this collection. But now that we are finally here... if I have learnt anything, and if I could pass on just one message to you, that is:

Write the story you wish others would tell. And that is what I did.

Yellow is my love letter to my culture. It is a celebration of my skin, my family and the beauty that comes with living between dual cultures. It is my way of saying thank you to the ones I love and goodbye to the trauma of my past. It is the preservation of memories and a hopeful nod to the future.

Most importantly, *Yellow* is for you. To all the kids who never got to see themselves in the stories they were told growing up. To my fellow creatives who fight for meaningful representation every day. And to every little child who will grow up to change the world. *I see you.* Your story is valid and my hope is that this will inspire you to tell it one day.

What has been mine for the last 22 years is now yours. Thank you for giving it a chance and I hope you take from it whatever you need to keep going on your own journey....

Love.
Chelsea

Chelsea Hui

I'm learning to love the hue of my skin,
To stop whispering my mother tongue like it's a secret,
To paint my life in shades of yellow.

Moonchild

I know you see by moonlight,
A kinder reality,
A different time,
But I promise,
You will find a place,
I promise,
We will remake this world together.

Bilingual

I am home to two countries,
Two cultures and countless conflicts,
Tell me,
What is more beautiful
than the amalgamation of both,
East and West,
On my tongue.

Feminine Form

Soft,
Uneven,
Luminescent,
Like the moon
this body has pulled tides,
And brought boys to their knees,
Who was it,
That taught us to shy away
from that kind of magic.

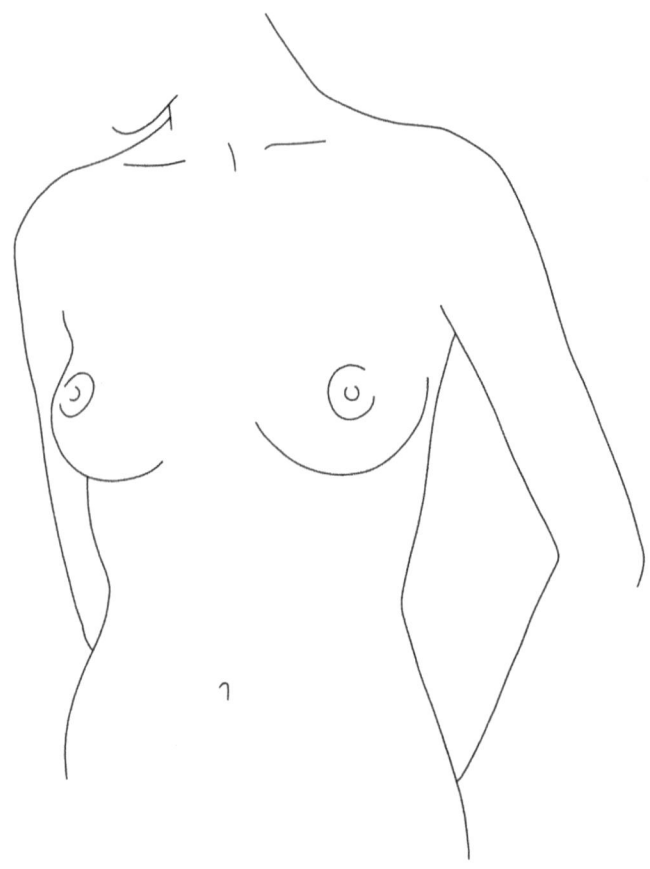

Chelsea Hui

Passing The Time

She is the poems that I write,
When sleep will not come.

Anxiety

Too many echoes in my mind,
Not enough air in my lungs.

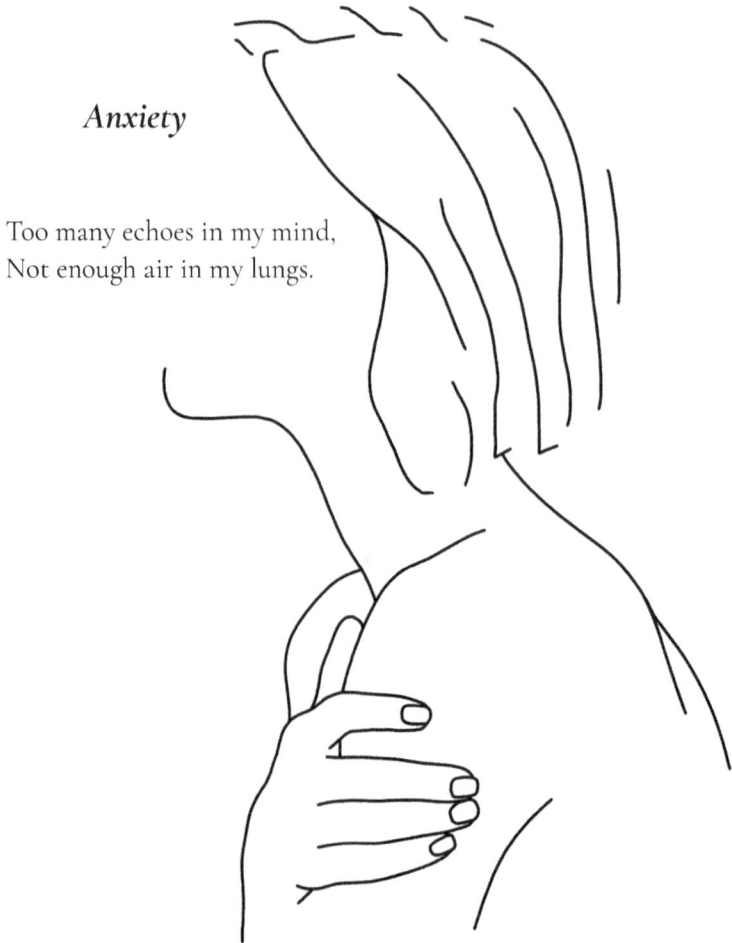

Chelsea Hui   cw: *Sexual Assault*

My Body, My Rules

When he pressures you
to prove your love,

      To show your dedication to him
      with your body,

            The only thing
            you need to show him,

                  Is the door.

Paperdoll

My life
is a collision of two cultures,
That never seemed to agree
on anything,
But my beauty,
On that,
They stand together,
To remind me
that my skin is dirty,
That it should be bleached,
To a cleaner,
Purer,
Shade of white,
Until
I
Fade

Chelsea Hui

Happily Ever After...

I grew up on fairytales,
Promising endings of love, of laughter,
Of princes and pumpkins,
Of happily ever afters,

Where the story was written by some other,
And set deeply in stone,
Where my path lead me to a knight in shining armour,
Who would *'save me'* from being alone,

But as I begin to experience my own truth,
I have found love is not all that they say,
It is not rigid nor judgemental,
And it can be found in so many ways,

I want tales where the princess falls in love,
Not with a prince, or a frog,
But where she realises 'twas a princess,
She really wanted all along,

Where she can decide,
To thrive standing on her own,
Where he can love who he wants,
Without needing others to condone,

To my future child,
Who may find themselves lost in the cold,
Who may not see any part of themselves,
In the stories they are told,

Promise me,
You will write your tale one of these days,
You will tell it to the world,
And live your life your own way.

Chelsea Hui

Love Is Love

I will not stop,
Until all love is held equal.

Chelsea Hui

Colour

It is intriguing how water colour runs
so seamlessly,
The trickle of water,
Into paint,
Into canvas,
A million different colours,
Bleeding together like Pacific sunset,
No harsh lines,
Free of division,
And it makes me wonder,
If we can learn to appreciate the incongruity of art,
Then we can most certainly learn to love
the diversity that is life.

My First Love

My heart aches for my mother always,
To hear the sound of her laugh,
The comfort in her words,
And to see the smile in her eyes,
No matter where I am in the world,
I am always homesick for her embrace,
To me,
She will always be home,
And no matter what I do,
I will always find my way back to her.

Change

You said I was afraid of change,
And you were right,
I was,
And I am,
Still I fear losing
myself,
And my reality,
In the pursuit of some
thing,
Already I am fading
along with the leaves,
Falling away from myself,
One piece at a time,
Until,
Just as I feared,
Nothing is as it was.

Chelsea Hui   cw: *Racism, Racial Slurs*

Chink

Chink,
Chink,
Like the sound of shovel to metal,
Buried beneath years of resentment
for our ancestors,
Who wore away upon your gold fields,
Left their families,
Homes,
To have their culture stripped,
Cut from the back of their heads,
And waved around like a prize,
Chink,
Like the sound of chains to bars,
The shackles my people
still cannot escape,
Chink.

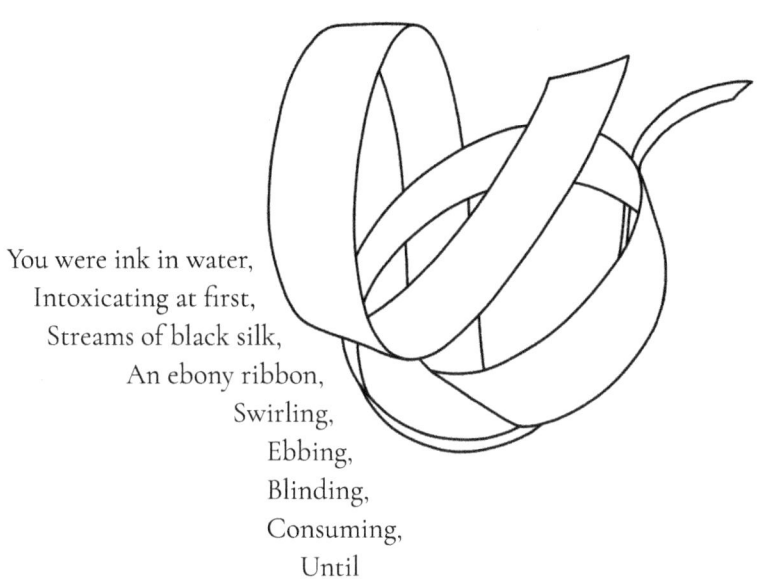

You were ink in water,
   Intoxicating at first,
     Streams of black silk,
        An ebony ribbon,
          Swirling,
           Ebbing,
          Blinding,
         Consuming,
         Until

there was nothing left.

Toxicity

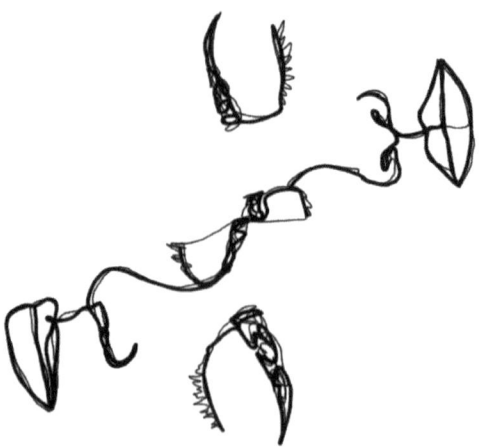

Humans or Whores

He wants a lady,
And a freak,
A saint,
And a whore,
Two sides of a coin,
That cannot exist without the other,
Two sides of a fantasy,
That cannot exist together.

Red String

You will find your way back to me,
The way the ocean fights to touch the shore again
each time it is pulled farther out,
Until then,
I will be here,
Waiting,
Until the tide rises again.

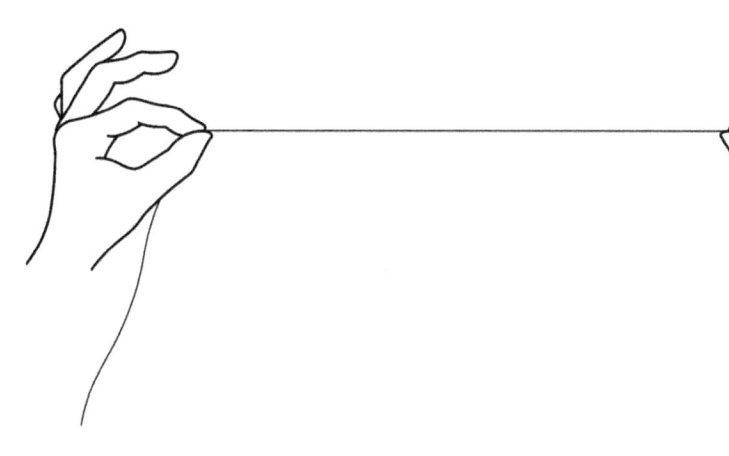

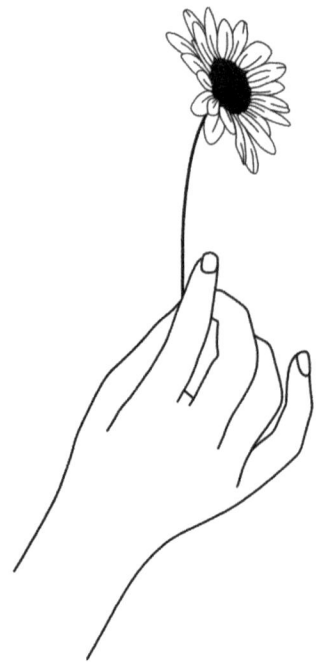

Intoxicated

When everything seemed wrong,
She found more comfort in the woods,
Amid the flowers and stones,
Than she ever did on those nights out,
Swallowing spirits and her own sanity.

Chelsea Hui

Climax

Your tongue is silk sliding over my collarbone,
Tickling my insides,
Ready to explode,
I want to climb under your skin
and draw the very life from inside you.

Chelsea Hui

Three Words, Eight Letters

Just three little words,
You whispered to my soul,
Our own perfect secret,
And like that,
You reached into my chest

and shook
my
fragile

heart.

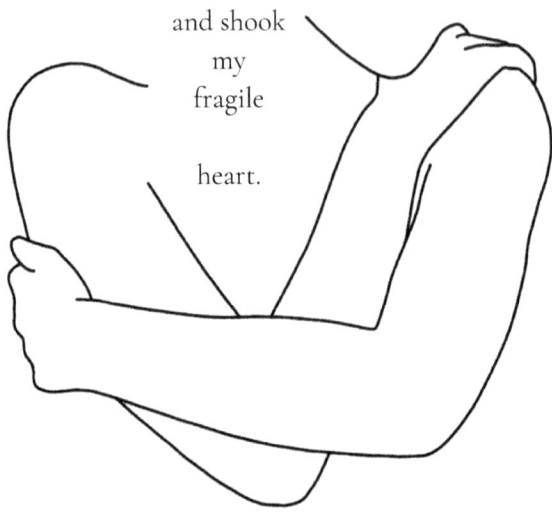

14.02.17

Gaslighting

The greatest disservice I did myself,
Was letting you convince me,
I was difficult to love,
That my heart,
That my mind,
That I,
Was anything short of enough.

cw: Racism

Yellow

My yellow,
Is a golden sunset,
Vast,
Endless,
As the possibilities my ancestors have fought to give me,

My yellow,
Is amber,
Hand-blown glass,
Beautiful,
And one of a kind,

My yellow,
Is not the yellow you paint me to be,
The yellow a young girl once saw in the mirror,
Skin dirty,
Eyes stretched into slits
as they ask her how she can see at all,

Nothing but an exotic face
and a quiet voice,
Silenced by your version of my story,
A fetish,
A joke,
One that I have heard you tell
far too many times,

My yellow is not yours,

My yellow is mine to reclaim,
My colour,
My body,
My culture,
My own.

Progress

It comes and goes in waves,
Each day as uncertain as the last,
Every step so fragile and so delicate,
And can too easily be shattered
by a single song,
Or a mere word.

   09. 08. 16

Insignificant

He plucked me from his mind,
As if I were nothing.

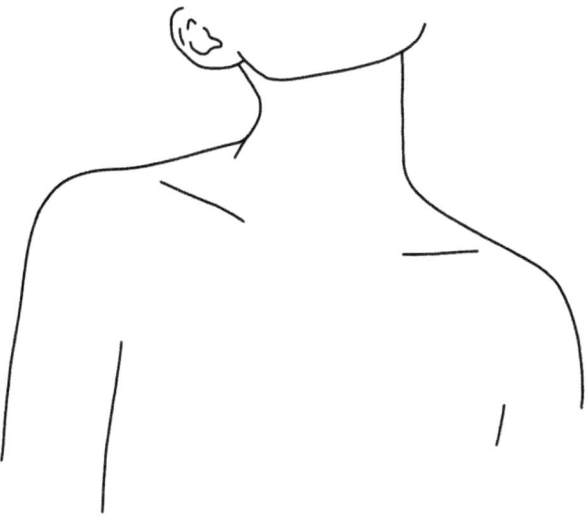

Wild & Free

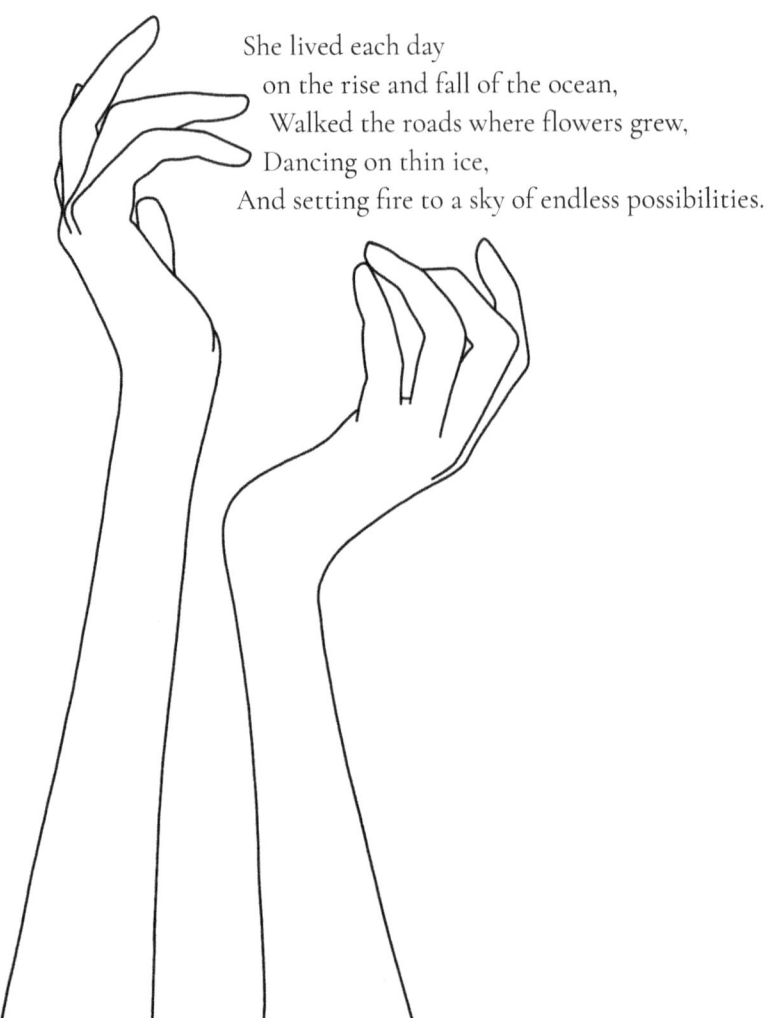

She lived each day
  on the rise and fall of the ocean,
    Walked the roads where flowers grew,
    Dancing on thin ice,
      And setting fire to a sky of endless possibilities.

Chelsea Hui   cw: Homophobia, Abuse

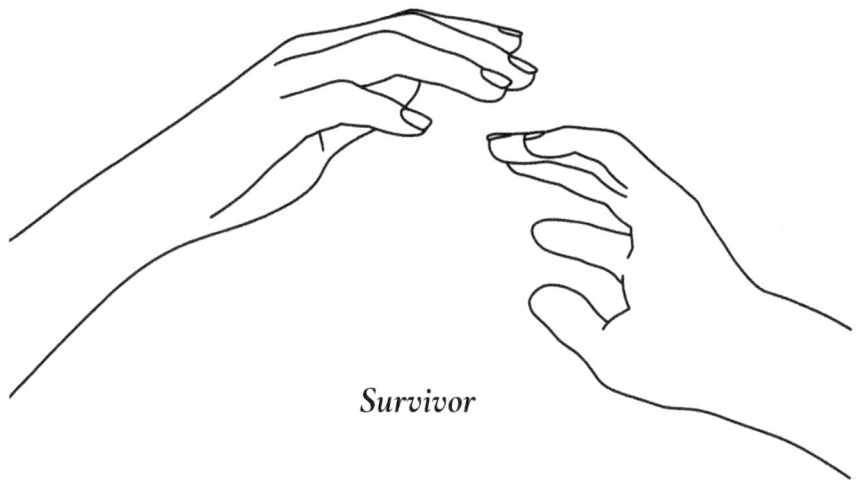

Survivor

I'm sorry this life has been cruel to you,
That your father beat the love out of you,
And your mother stood silent,
No one
deserves to be treated as you were,
Because of where their love lies.

Chelsea Hui   cw: *Sexual Assault*

A Memory

Your memory
is a locked car door,
Torn clothes,
Stuffy air,
Your memory is a smear,
Like blood on white linen,
Bleach on bare skin,
You will be remembered
as a criminal,
Now you tell me,
Does that feel good?

Chelsea Hui

*I don't want to dislike myself anymore,
She finally said.*

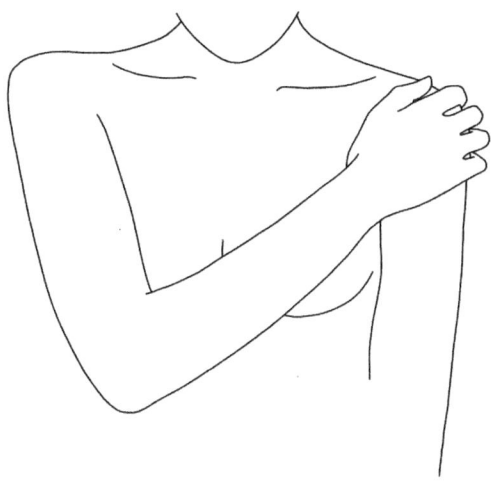

cw: Sexism

Baby Girl

A boy,
Please,
They whispered to my pregnant mother,
A whisper,
Loud enough to ignite a fire in her belly,
A force of nature,
Who would grow up
to burn their expectations to the ground,
And bloom,
Like the fighter she is.

Chelsea Hui

The Most Beautiful Moment In Life

Today
you are younger than you will be
                      tomorrow
                      you will be one step closer,

                      We are young,
                      We are reckless,
                      And we are far too alive,
                      To turn back already.

Spirited Away

My heart aches at the thought of it,
Gates,
Leading through tunnels,
That should take me home,
Or what now feels like a home away from home,
As the trail of goodbyes linger behind me,
I count the steps,
Further and further,

Until we meet again.

Chelsea Hui

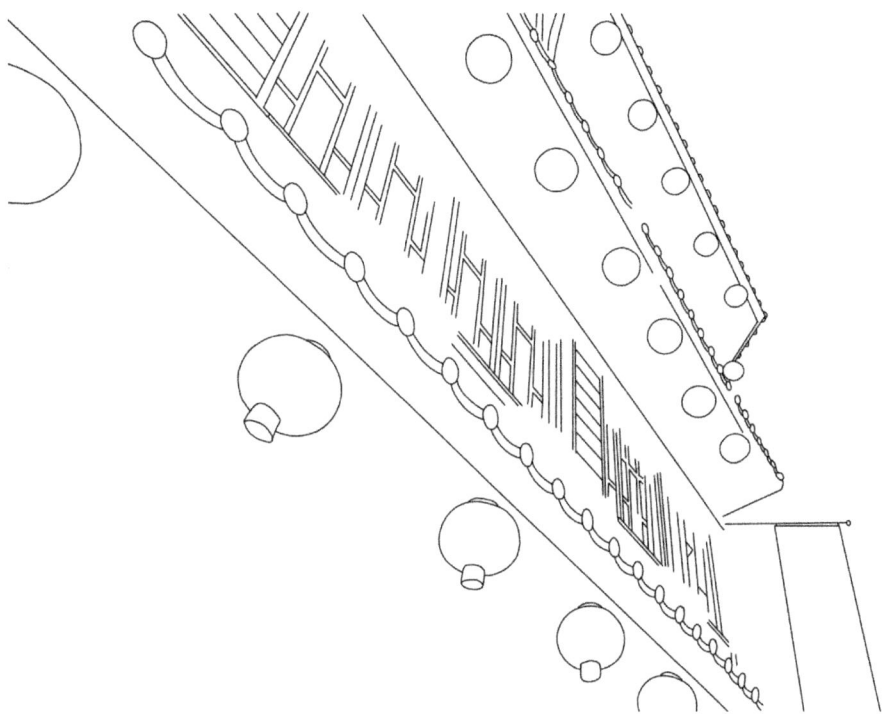

To The Women Of My Life

They may stay quiet,
May seem meek,
But they are warriors of peace,
Fighting every day
to protect this home,
At war with tempers and tantrums,
Responding only in patience and poise,
When I search for strength and humility,
It has a face,
My mother's,
My grandma's,
They are women of a different time,
Women with more knowledge and power
than I will ever know.

Chelsea Hui

Gone

My heart cries I miss you,
My body pleads I want you,
My mind screams I need you,

And yet,
That isn't enough,

And it never will be again.

03.03.15

A Perfect Illusion

We let our demons play in the dark,
Nurturing poison with passion,
You were the first to dance with my shadows,
Who saw through the smoke
and the smog,

But all of it,

Everything between us,

This relationship,

Was built
on insecurities,

It was a love

built

on mutual destruction.

Chelsea Hui   *cw: Sexual Assault*

Carrying Your Shame

He left a mark on me,
A shame
I cannot shake,
A bruise between my legs
that never really fades,
Some nights I wake up,
And I can still taste the aggression,
From when he forced his lips against mine,
Cutting my voice off like barbed wire,
I have had to teach my body,
That your touch,
Is nothing like his was,
Coarse
against my throbbing skin,
And I have learnt that he is the only one to blame,
For his crimes have nothing to do with me,
Or what I was wearing.

Chelsea Hui

White Noise

My world is a reminder of your presence,
Everywhere I turn, everywhere I look,
Are echoes of sweet kisses and
whispers of a promised future,
Of nights spent tangled in limbs
and warmth and love,
And the relics of a past life,
There's a hollow pain that eats away the day
and swallows me up at night,
And then there's nothing,
Nothing but white noise,
And all the mess is drowned out
by numbness and blank walls in my mind.

04.08.16

Chelsea Hui

許

That day
I told myself,
Never again,
I carved my family name onto my chest,
And wore it proudly as my crest,
I did it so that I would remember,

That day
I promised myself,
I would never let anyone make me feel ashamed,
Of my name,
My family,
Or my culture,
Ever again.

(Inspired by Kimmy Yam)

Just Stay Gone

The day you left,

I mopped the floor clean of the excuses

you left

trailing

behind you,

Across states,

Like you were sprinkling

breadcrumbs,

for me

to follow.

Father

You taught me that toughness,
And kindness,
Are not mutually exclusive,
Throughout my life,
You have shown me both,
And for that,
I thank you.

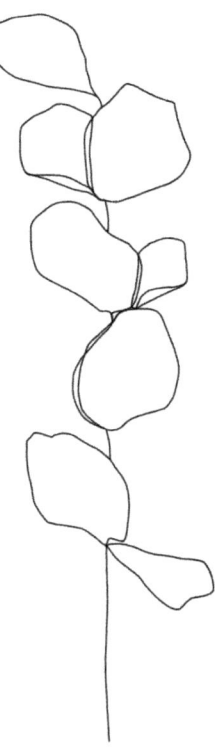

Emotional Affairs

I told you we were just friends,
Which was mostly true,
And while we never touched,
Or loved the way you feared we would,
He had touched my mind
and my soul,
In ways you could never have imagined.

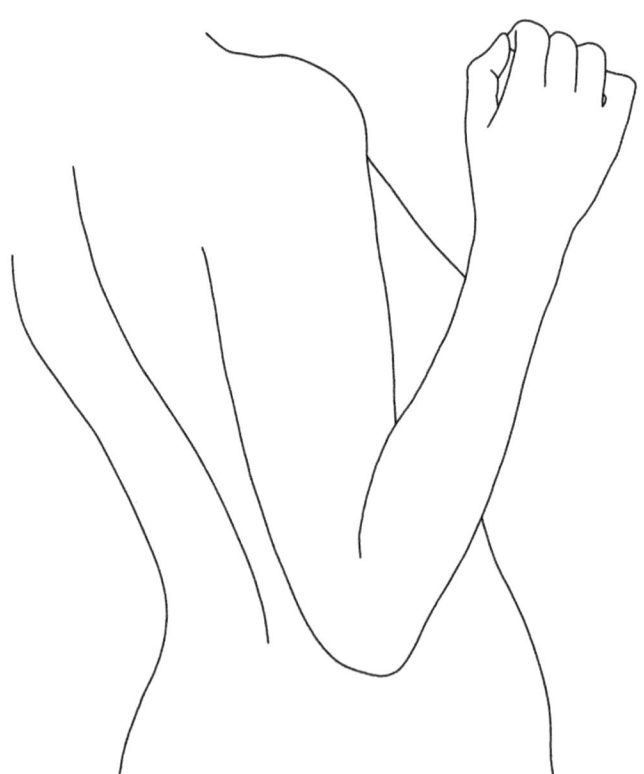

Chelsea Hui

These Eyes Of Mine

I have hated them,
Abused them,
These eyes of mine,
The eyes of my father,
My ancestors,
The eyes of my culture.

Designer

Go back to your country,
Say the same people,
Who take my cultural dress,
And wear it as a fashion statement.

Chelsea Hui

I'm Learning How To Love Myself

I put my love where it did not belong,
Because it was easier,
To lose myself in your eyes,
Than to look myself in the mirror,
And search for the love I was missing.

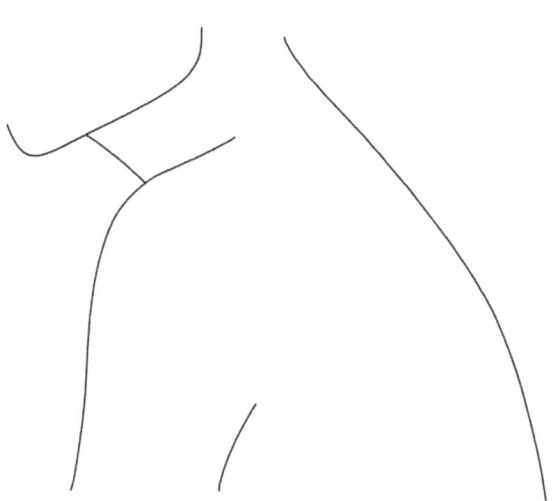

Chelsea Hui

Remember Me

You are evaporating before my eyes,
Like grey smoke into crisp air,
What once burnt cities to the ground
is now faded,
Distant,
You are a memory I crave,

I need,
I must,
I will,

Remember,

Remember,

Remember,

That is my promise to you.

Chelsea Hui

Say Something

I was in a relationship,
But most of the time,

I was alone.

When I think of the past,

Your face is the one that I see,

All the things we said and promised,

When we were once happy,

I juggle the possibilities,

A world that can never be,

A life free from this regret,

Of what we could have been,

But what about you?

What is it that you see?

When the past comes flooding back,

Do you even think of me?

The Thoughts I Think At 2am

Chelsea Hui

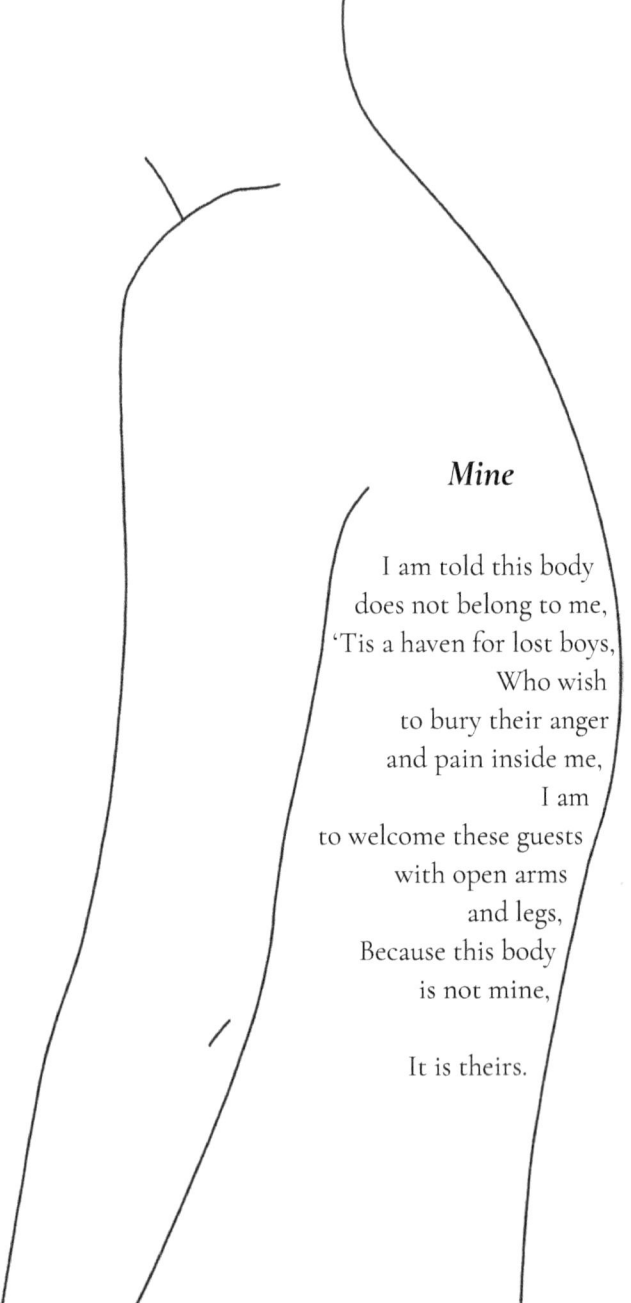

Mine

I am told this body
does not belong to me,
'Tis a haven for lost boys,
Who wish
to bury their anger
and pain inside me,
I am
to welcome these guests
with open arms
and legs,
Because this body
is not mine,

It is theirs.

Chelsea Hui

Hong Kong, I Love You

You can break my bones,
Take back my freedom,
But my spirit is not in this soil,
It is etched into my being,
It is with the youth of my city,
Scattered on these sidewalks
night after night,
My soul is eternal,
Stretched across this skyline
from my shore to my peak,
My body may be yours,
For now,
But my mind is free,
And it will live on
to carve our stories into history.

Chelsea Hui   *cw: Graphic*

Alone Together

Your body only inches above mine,
Hands roaming,
Breath catching,
Lips parting,
Every part of our bodies was close,
And yet,
Somehow,

I had never felt more alone.

Chelsea Hui

The One That Got Away

I come to you in the middle of the night,
As the moonlight kisses your eyelids,
Remember when I did that?
The trails of twilight linger down your spine,
A reminder of where my fingers once were,
No matter where you are,
Or who she is,
I am here,
Above you like the night sky,
A forever constant,
I am the dusk to your dawn,
I am nightfall,
And no matter how high the sun rises,
It will still fall,
Night will always come.

Chelsea Hui

*All the hurt in this world
makes me feel extremely lucky,
And incredibly guilty,
All at once.*

All For Love

When I found you,
I had hope that you saw me,
Heard me,
That you might rescue me from the darkest parts inside,
Mend the cuts I had put there myself,

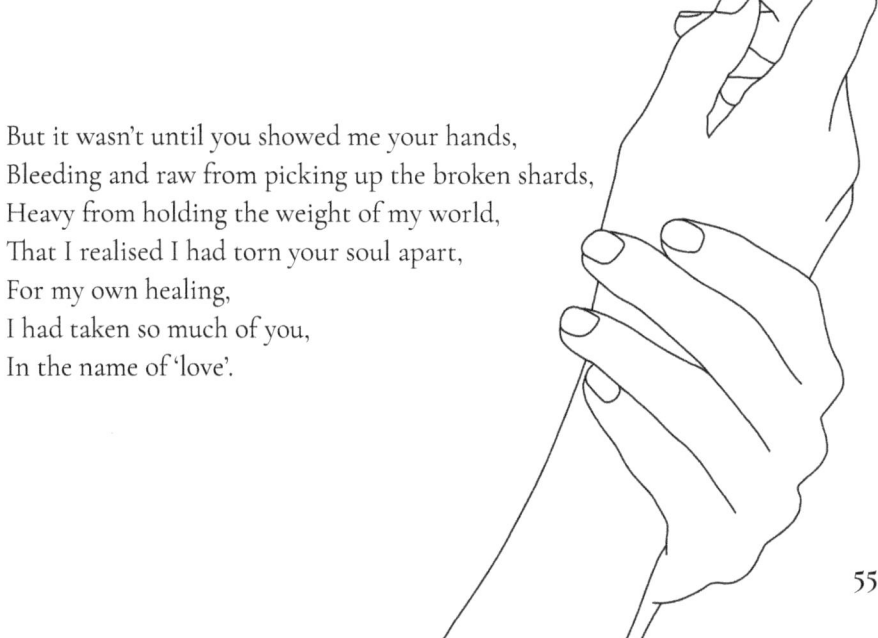

But it wasn't until you showed me your hands,
Bleeding and raw from picking up the broken shards,
Heavy from holding the weight of my world,
That I realised I had torn your soul apart,
For my own healing,
I had taken so much of you,
In the name of 'love'.

Strength

Make no mistake,
He did not break me,
No one,
No one possesses that kind of power.

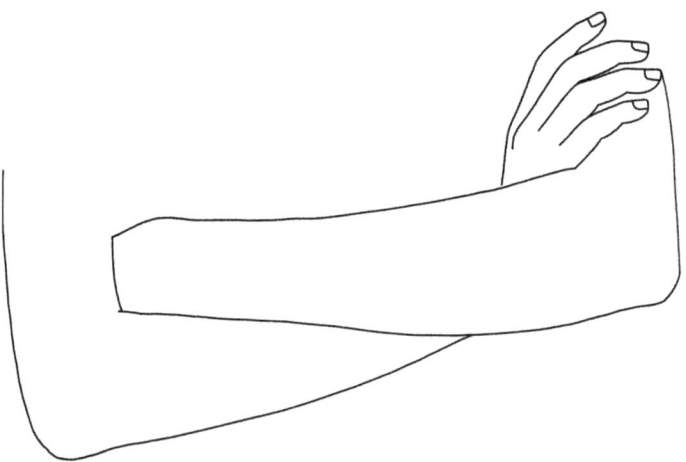

爷爷 *(Grandfather)*

I think of him
when it rains,

Eyes clamped shut,
Longing for some peace,
Before he has to get up
and do it all again,

Underneath his body,
The pavement is his bed,
And his bare hands,
A pillow
for him to rest his head,

As the dawn breaks,
He picks himself up,
Dusts off the rain,
Soaked into his beaten bones,
And does it all over again.

My Life Long Partner

This body is a memoir,
Nights marked down by lovers,
Relished days under the sun,
Kisses from my mother,
Scuffles with my sister,
It carries love stories,
And battle scars,
It has served me,
Protected me,
Loved me,
Patiently waiting
for me to return the favour.

Chelsea Hui

The One That Came Before Me

I am scared to love you completely,
For fear I might have to taste the words
you once spoke to her,
Words that still linger on your lips
each time we speak of the past,
To confront the harshest reality,
That maybe,
I am living here,
In her shadow,

I have let you swim in every inch of my waters,
Letting you bathe in the deepest
and sometimes darkest pools of my mind,
Yet when it comes to you,
There are still oceans of unchartered territory,
That you may never let me explore,

I see her,
The ghost of your past,
Swimming behind your eyes
when you look into mine,
And the fingerprints she left
along the walls of your heart,
Red and soiled with her selfish desires,

So when you are ready to let me in,
I promise,
I will not do as she did,
Time and time again,
And take your delicate heart for granted,
And in turn,
I pray you will not bruise mine.

Chelsea Hui

In His Place

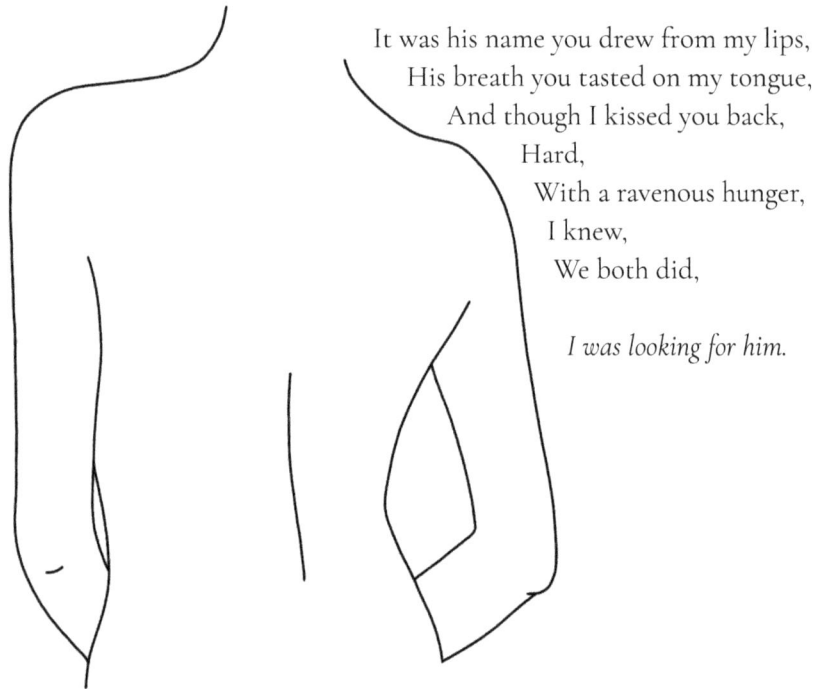

It was his name you drew from my lips,
His breath you tasted on my tongue,
And though I kissed you back,
Hard,
With a ravenous hunger,
I knew,
We both did,

I was looking for him.

Chelsea Hui

Nostalgia

It was like a flash of the past,

In a sea of strangers,

And when he hugged me

and asked how I'd been,

I felt the peace I've been searching for,

Maybe this is how we were meant to be all along.

Chelsea Hui

Hush

Listen,
Listen as she whispers,
Her stories,
They bear a pain
you cannot understand,
Cannot fathom,
So listen,
For her voice,
Her whisper,
Is how we will catch the monsters.

Morning Wonderings

It is 5:00am,
Outside my window
the world is asleep,
Still and not yet tainted
by the dank smell
of schedules and flurried minds,
Rushing from destination
to appointment,
Unaware of the precious time
that is passing them by,

It is 5:00am,
And I lay here,
Awake and untouched
by the expectations
that lurk outside my door,
And each silent second that passes
is like music to my ears,

It is 5:00am,
I watch idly as the dawn descends,
Covering the sea of rooftops
like a blanket of light,
Then suddenly everything
is in slow-motion,
And my mind is at peace,

Because it is 5:00am,
And outside my window,
The world is a spectacle.

Chelsea Hui

Love with you made the rest feel easy

My Soulmate

What others spend a lifetime seeking,
I found on the day I was born,
A partner for life,
Someone to call my rock,
A soulmate,
A sister.

Chelsea Hui

These days,
I feel as though I live in the furrow
between your brows,
In the arc of your lips,
The confusion in your eyes,
Some days,
No matter how hard I try,
My emotions seem to be lost on you.

Miscommunication

Firefighter

When I look into my mother's eyes,
I see kindness,
The kindness she teaches me to carry,
The kindness you taught her,
Each time I look into her eyes,
I see you.

Chelsea Hui

Sweater Weather

A cocoon of warmth
surrounds our bodies,
A sanctuary,
To shield the cold breath around us,
Your fingers feel like warm syrup,
Slipping over my belly,
Then my back,
To my face,
I smile,
Ease into the hands that hold me,
And breathe in the brisk scent of autumn.

Chelsea Hui

Linger

When the lights go dim,

And the music turns silent,

That's when the mind wanders

to places it shouldn't,

Places too far for comfort.

Empty Words

Lately,
When
she
says
I love you,

I
know
what
she
really
means
is
I'm sorry,

And
those
three
words,
Words
that
I
once
craved
to
hear,

Now taste dirty on her lips.

Hourglass

This body is an hourglass,
Counting down the years
until it goes stale,
Watching my youth slip away,
One grain at a time,
And as the last one falls,
I promise I will smile
for it was nothing,
Nothing but casing for your passion,
A chamber for your intelligence,
A shell for your creativity,
Your body will wither,
No creams or fad diets
will change that,
But the people,
The laughter,
The story,
Those will stand,
Those are forever.

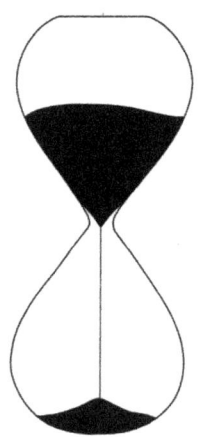

History

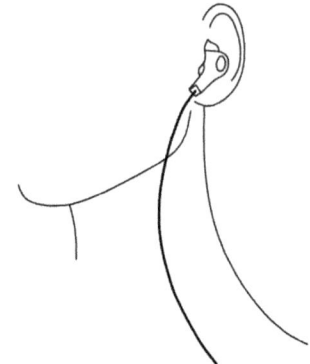

That song has been on repeat

    since the day you left,

        The bridge,

      It paves a path to you,

Takes me closer than I have been,

        In months.

I Am A Writer...

I used your tears as the ink in my pen,
I took your pain
and recreated it,
In some attempt to escape my own,

I have found peace in these half truths,
And I hate myself for that,
I hate myself for it,
and I am sorry.

Amy

She was a girl,
Born of the wrong era,
A woman,
Ahead of her time,
Misunderstood,
Mocked for her spirit,
Her drive,
To the strongest woman in my life,
Know that the best parts of me,
My boldness,
My fire,
They are in my blood,
They are your greatest gift to me.

Foundation Of Success

Your success does not depend on her failures,
Her achievement is not your downfall,
If only we were not taught to think so.

Chelsea Hui

And Then There Were Three

There are those who come and go,
Those who walk with you for as long as they can,
Until the path splits,
Those who try
and try and try,
Until they can't,

Then there are those who will beat the storm,
Who will carve their names
into the walls of your temple,
Written and bound in gold,
Who will build forts and castles
with you,

Among the many faces we meet,
There are those special few,
That understand,
Protect,
With all they have,
Faces,
You can never let go.

You have me undone,
Quivering,
At your touch,
Nothing,
Has ever tasted so sweet.

Desire

Chelsea Hui

Daughters

A boy is what they wanted,
Two warriors are what they got.

Chelsea Hui

Wings

We are but birds,
Stuck in the cages of our own making,

I have been waiting to unclip myself, of
fear, of
judgement, of
pain,

To spread these wings,
And finally take myself
where I've always wanted to go.

Acceptance

The day I realised that life,
Is less about
perfection,
And more about
authenticity,

Is the day
I was
set
free.

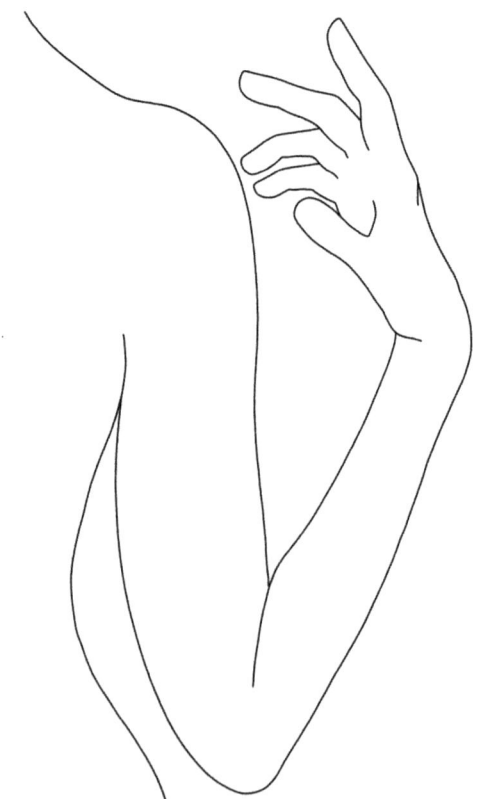

Chelsea Hui

I'm The One I Should Love

I have learnt to love myself

far too deeply,

For me to allow anyone else

to do it half-heartedly.

The One

She knew he was the end,
End of the comings,
End of the goings,
He was the end
to end all endings.

Perspective

She cried every night,
Losing her mind over blurry details
and hopeful fantasies,
Desperate to move on,
Yet terrified of letting it all go,

But when it was finally over,
From her cheeks,
She brushed aside the trails of pain,
And looked at the world with new eyes,
Fresh with the flicker of possibility.

Chelsea Hui

Burn

Don't you dare dim that flame
for someone who turned away,
Because they couldn't handle your heat,
You are fire,
Meant to blaze trails
and bring light to this world,
You are fire,
And you were not born to be contained.

For Alexander

Loving you
is like the smell of rain
before the storm,
It is pure happiness
and complete chaos,
Feeling blissful in your arms
after shouting our chords raw,
Loving you is everything,
And could too easily be nothing,
To love you,
Is to love in extremes.

Chelsea Hui

Enough

You were before him,
And you will be after him.

Self-Worth

What a thing it is
to be living at all,
Beneath the courtship
of the sun and the moon,
Amongst the flowers,
The trees,
And all your blemishes,
This life is a gift,
This world is a blessing,
And your very existence is a goddamn miracle.

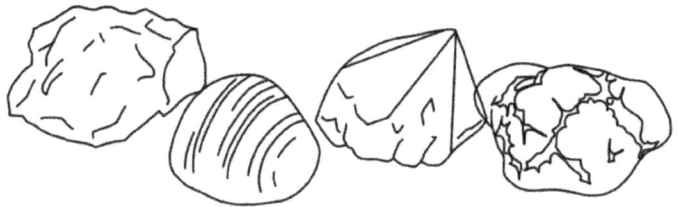

Chelsea Hui

My Story

I want to tell my story,
To write about the softness of his bedsheets,
The way the cotton falls against my back,
The wrinkles on her hands,
Carved deep with their own journeys,
I want to write about our truths,
Our reality,
The gentle,
And the unjust,
I want to write about it all,
Because it is in the details,
The pleasure,
The trauma,
The love,
This is my story,
A story from me to you.

Acknowledgements:

Thank you to my artist, Tanya Scott. I count my blessings everyday for the series of misfortunes that eventually led me to you. I am eternally grateful for your kindness, your generosity, and your incredible talent.

To Janice, my 姐姐, my pumpkin. Every step I take into the world is to follow the trail you have blazed for me. So much of this book was created on those long train trips going up to visit you, and something about that seems so meant to be.

To my incredible parents. Everything I am is because of your sacrifice. Thank you for giving me my life and the opportunity to chase my passions. I love you - the kindness you have taught me has carried me through everything.

And finally, thank you to all of you - my dear readers. I can't begin to express how surreal it is to receive so much love and kindness from people I have never met before. Please know that I appreciate every single one of you. Thank you for putting your faith in my words and I hope that your journey with *Yellow* was everything you needed it to be.

Find Chelsea here

 *chelseahui.com*

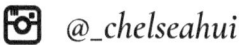 *@_chelseahui*

Find Tanya here

 @thecolourstudy

CPSIA information can be obtained
at www.ICGtesting.com
Printed in the USA
BVHW020813160520
579798BV00021B/1269